About the Author

Malcolm Allen was raised in Aldershot, joined the army, and enjoyed a varied military career which took him to many countries. Along the way he married Jill but ten years, nine moves and two daughters later he resigned for a second career in industry. Later, he took early retirement and was recruited to run the Hertfordshire County Show. Malcolm lives with his wife in Berkhamsted not too close to their five grandchildren.

Dedication

To Jake, Alfie, Harry, Rosie and Sam, whom I love dearly.

Malcolm Allen

STANDING OPERATING PROCEDURES FOR GRANDFATHERS

AUSTIN MACAULEY
PUBLISHERS LTD.

A CIP catalogue record for this title is available from the British Library.

ISBN 978 1 78554 964 9 (Paperback)
ISBN 978 1 78554 965 6 (Hardback)

www.austinmacauley.com

First Published (2015)
Austin Macauley Publishers Ltd.
25 Canada Square
Canary Wharf
London
E14 5LQ

Printed and bound in Great Britain

Acknowledgements

To all the other grandparents who do a great job. Don't take this personally!

INTRODUCTION

The British Army is one of the few remaining British institutions that is both respected and effective. This situation has not come about by accident; it is all down to leadership, training and carefully evolved principles and procedures. I make no excuse, therefore, for applying these same principles and procedures to the role of grandfather.

Grandchildren are extremely valuable commodities and so are grandfathers. Both parties will benefit from a harmonious and close relationship from day 1. (See note 1)

In normal operations there are usually two grandfathers and this can complicate issues, particularly if one grandfather:
A. Lives closer to the grandchild than the other.
B. Has a beard or other traditional comforting features akin to a comfortable lap or knitting in the female equivalent, the grandmother.
C. Is wealthier

The aim of this manual is to set out the structure that will ensure a clear and loving relationship between a grandparent and a grandchild. (See note 2)

NB. Abbreviations have been kept to a minimum but to avoid confusion a short glossary of useful terms can be found at the end of this book.

Notes:
1. The date of birth of the grandchild.
2. Reference to grandchild can mean grandson or granddaughter.

1st Principle

Selection and Maintenance of the Aim

This is the first principle of war and should also be the first principle of grandfathership. In every grandfather to grandchild (GF/GC) relationship it is essential that from the start, the grandfather has a single, unambiguous objective which he must stick with, no matter what circumstances prevail.

THAT AIM IS:

TO BE THE FAVOURITE GRANDFATHER!

No 'ifs', no 'buts', no wobbling - do it!

3

2nd Principle

Maintenance of Morale

The morale (see note 3) referred to is that of the grandfather and it can easily be destroyed, mainly by the grandchild (G/C). High morale is guaranteed at each first meeting but can rapidly decline as the hours pass and the 'little personality' of the G/C is expressed. A determined grandfather will be responsive to developments while still maintaining the aim.

Morale can be restored in the following ways:
1. Restricting the length of visits.
2. Retiring at intervals during longer visits.
3. Feigning illness thus gaining sympathy.
4. Plenty of grog.

Never try to improve morale by correcting G/C or making behavioural suggestions within earshot of parents, the grandmother (G/M) or the other grandparents (TOGPs).

Finally, no matter how exhausted you are, always ensure that all departures are effusive and that any expletives and cries of relief are delayed until you are well out of earshot.

Morale can be restored!

Notes:
3. Morale is the degree of mental or moral confidence in an individual or group. High morale is hugely dependent on a successful campaign.

3rd Principle

Offensive Action

This principle determines the practical ways a grandfather seeks to gain advantage over TOGPs or, indeed, any other relation, how he must act in order to sustain the momentum of that advantage and, finally, to seize the initiative. Fair play does not come into this but outright denigration of other contenders should be avoided. Children are not stupid. (see note 4)

Intelligence and information are essential factors in gaining the advantage. Know what other contenders are buying as presents or what trips they are planning and get in first. Disinformation is a useful weapon and recommendations can be made about wonderful places to take grandchildren. Recommend those which you know are awful, crowded, expensive, or which shut with little notice.

The downside of gaining the advantage is that it has to be sustained and this will involve sacrifice and expense. If this tends to distract from the maintenance of the aim then show some intestinal fortitude for God's sake.

Finally it should be understood that grandchildren are adept at offensive action because that is the way children are.

Do not let them rile you!

Note:
4. Well, some are.

4th Principle

Security

No commander is pleased if the secrets of his plans and dispositions are revealed. We know too that small children have big ears (see note 5) and we must watch what we say. However, in the grandfather campaign security is more concerned with personal hygiene, a consideration that some of us elderly gentlemen find challenging at times. Remember that G/C live in a waist level underworld and spend a lot of time looking upwards.

Children are very 'pass remarkable' and will unashamedly tell you that you smell, you have hairs in your ears and you have a bogey up your nose! These candid observations can hurt, but they can be embarrassing when uttered in public places where the usual resigned, apologetic smile to members of the public will have no value whatsoever.

Planning is the answer and grandfathers must be impeccable about personal hygiene. Out must go those trusty corduroy slacks and that stained favourite jumper. Underwear must be changed daily or more often in some circumstances. Think about resupply. Invest in electric nose and ear clippers, a good aftershave (it is not effeminate to use one) and don't be offended when your nose is compared with that of a certain monkey at the zoo.

Swallow the pain, remember the aim!

Note 5: 'Big ears' refers not to the physical size of the otic organ but rather to its ability to tune into words that it should not hear. Conversely G/Cs ears have a filter which prevents them heeding instructions and commands, no matter how often repeated or the decibel level of the transmission.

9

5th Principle

Surprise

Surprise is one of the most important weapons that a commander has at his disposal. The introduction of the unexpected usually results in shock and confusion, which can then be exploited. It is the same with the GF/GC relationship. The unexpected present or treat is always a good ploy (see note 6) but, if repeated too often, it will soon be received with blasé indifference or, worse, score a point for the enemy: 'the other grandpa took us there last week!' Be careful.

Surprise is also a two-sided weapon so be prepared to be stopped in your tracks at any time. Mood swings are de rigueur with small children and they are quick to show them. Ignorance of the names and characteristics of favourite things can cause loss of face and the inability to perform reasonably well on iPad games can be disastrous.

As a minimum:
1. Know the opening words to the song from Frozen
2. Be able to identify the goodies and baddies in Star Wars and name at least six characters.
3. Be adept at Lego and Angry Birds.
4. Know what channel Cbeebies is on.
5. Be able to build a wall using Minecraft.

If you are surprised, don't be exploited!

Note:
6: A ploy is a cunningly devised deliberation aimed at gaining an underhand advantage.

6th Principle

Concentration of Force

This rule involves the synchronised application of power to reinforce the intended effect. But hang on grandfathers. Forget about the days when you controlled the behaviour of your own children by chastisement, sometimes 'reinforcing the effect' with a pinking slap on a chubby thigh. That's a no no now (see note 7) regrettably, but even so and most importantly it would not advance the aim.

Concentration of force here is about using everything and everybody at your disposal to further your cause. Remind Granny, indirectly, to reinforce your position at every opportunity. Ensure that friends who meet your grandchildren treat them nicely and blitz them with your good points. Always be extra friendly to your G/Cs friends even though they may be the most ghastly and insolent miniature sub-humans you have ever come across. Finally, don't omit the person who has more effect on your little darlings than anyone else in the world including, perhaps, their mother. I refer of course to Miss Goody, the primary school teacher.

When dropping off your G/C be sure to butter up Miss G. Praise the school, her projects, say how much she is loved by the children and thank her enthusiastically for the benefits she brings to your G/C, the country, the world, the universe, etc. You cannot be too ingratiating as I observed this method being successfully employed by a number of rising stars in the army.

Brownnosing Pays!

Notes:
7. A 'no no' is a euphemism for 'forbidden' or 'beyond the pale.' For example it is a 'no no' to open a door for a lady these days, apparently!

7th Principle

Economy of Effort

This is best defined as the judicious exploitation of all resources in the successful pursuit of the objective. Most commanders have limited resources and, without exception, always want more. Grandfathers are usually well resourced so this principle really does not apply.

Go immediately to the next principle!

8th Principle

Flexibility

'Your flexible friend' was the slogan of the Access credit card with which we became familiar between 1972 and 1996 and, yes, a credit card is a necessity for successful grandparenting, especially when the little ones grow bigger. In business too, the ability to change to meet new circumstances is hugely important. But the flexibility demanded by young grandchildren is more physical.

Games are played at carpet level and if you wish to curry favour by pushing Thomas and his friends (see note 9) around the track you have to get down there with them. Flexible fingers are required with Lego and other expensive and fiddly toys and the stresses that are put on your body assisting in the play park are huge. What is your heart rate like after pushing a solemn one year old on a swing for twenty minutes? Be aware too that a quiet sit down on the sofa with the paper doesn't guarantee recovery time. No, for then you become the target for running jumps, hurled building blocks and discarded cups and bottles.

My advice is to keep fit. Try yoga or the gym two or three times a week. Then there is always the desperation standby; 'Granny is very good at that game'.

Don't try break dancing

Note:
9. For new or aspiring grandfathers 'Thomas and his friends' refers to some unworldly stories of humanoid trains written by a vicar some years ago. Know the names of the main locomotives and note that political correctness in the US and TV versions has resulted in the replacement of the Fat Controller by Sir Topham Hatt.

9th Principle

Cooperation

Now this is a tricky one chaps because cooperation is all about team work and sharing the load, qualities which are contrary to our aim. Too much teamwork waters down the effort you are making to ingratiate yourself into the minds of the enemy, the grandchildren I mean. However, if you are cunning, assistance with sharing the burden is a worthwhile thing to do. Take looking after the brood for a day. There will be plenty of opportunities to demonstrate your kindness, spoil them, jump to their every call but use every opportunity to bow out when you calculate that effort outweighs reward. Then the teamwork can begin. Grannies are useful tools at this time but also remember that TV, video, and crayons help to reduce the load. A treasure hunt is also an excellent time passer, but make it difficult so that they stay in the garden a long time. Don't forget young families living near you can be drawn into the campaign as well. Don't be shy in suggesting a play date with the young family who have just moved in.

Cooperation with TOGPs is best avoided!

10th Principle

Sustainability

All the foregoing advice is pretty valueless if the principles are applied irregularly or in such a way that the advantages that you have gained are dissipated through lack of planning or an error. It is important to ensure that all your actions can be maintained reasonably comfortably so that the freedom to do what you must is maintained. To be the favourite grandfather nothing should become 'old hat' but neither must you get yourself into a corner. Have alternatives to 'The Galloping Major' as this favourite will wear thin as you and the grandchildren get older. A present should not be expected at every visit but when one is given it should have some wow factor. Remember too that a trip to the play park is not to ensure the little ones have fun but rather to exhaust them so that you can get some peace and quiet that evening.

You'll be lucky
and
GOOD LUCK!

SOPs for Grandfathers

A Glossary of Useful Terms

Bath time - A getting wet experience.

Bedtime - An exercise in juvenile procrastination.

Cushion - A decorative, soft fabric support item for throwing on the floor.

Dining table - A receptacle for discarded food.

Discipline - An extinct word.

Drum - Don't even consider it.

Excrement - See Snot.

Family holiday - One or two weeks of hell.

Family gathering - A shorter period of hell.

Family meal - A frantic and hazardous occasion. A dry cleaner's delight.

Garden - A jungle training area.

Grandfather - A kind, generous and mature gentleman who worries more about his grandchildren than he did about his own children.

Grandmother - The PA to the grandfather.

Grandchildren - The 'adorable' offspring of the grandfather's children.

Humour - What children find funny. This mainly involves bodily functions, rude noises and smells.

iPad - An electronic gadget that can be operated by grandchildren better than grandparents. A constant source of argument if there is more than one grandchild.

Nappy (Diaper US) - Something grandfathers must ignore.

Nappy (a dirty one) - Something grandfathers must avoid.

Not well - A minor or passing complaint or illness which causes grandfathers anxiety when Google'd.

Nursery school - An academy of sticking, painting and singing. Also a respite centre for mothers.

Parents - Youngish people under stress.

Personality - An annoying trait exhibited by a grandchild when it doesn't get its way.

Play Park - An aid station for grandparents where they can discuss grandchildren with other grandparents. See also retribution.

Present or gift - A carefully chosen object which is received ungraciously and quickly discarded.

Retribution - A constant grandfatherly thought.

Sofa - A trampoline.

School - A place with insufficient car parking.

Snot - An excretion easily and often transferred from child to grandfather.

Smart Phone - A small telephone that grandchildren like to throw and which grandfathers can't be bothered with.

Smart arse - An older grandchild.

Stick - A desired object that must be collected.

Tidy-up - An event that never happens.

TOGPs - Space intrusive pseudo relations.

Toys - Expensive, mainly plastic, baubles found on the floor.

Twacks - Things that twains and twams wun on.